Themesongs

Hymns for every Sunday,
major Festivals and Holy Days
in the Alternative Service Book

Texts by
Michael Forster

Kevin Mayhew

First published in Great Britain in 1993 by

KEVIN MAYHEW LTD
Rattlesden
Bury St Edmunds
Suffolk IP30 0SZ

Phone 0449 737978

ISBN 0 86209 466 6

© Copyright 1993 by Kevin Mayhew Ltd.

The hymns in this book are protected by copyright and may not be reproduced in any way for sale or private use without the consent of the copyright owner.

Cover design by Juliette Clarke
Printed and bound in Great Britain

Foreword

The hymns in *Themesongs* have been written to reflect the unity of the Sunday readings in the *Alternative Service Book*. They add to the continuity, development and understanding of the liturgy and can be sung at any suitable part of the Service.

All the hymns are set to well-known hymn tunes so that they can be sung without rehearsal and with confidence, making 128 new hymns instantly accessible to congregations.

A list of suggested tunes is given at the back of this edition; for example, the suggested tune for hymn number 1, for the 9th Sunday before Christmas, is *All through the night (Ar hyd y nos)*, although any melody of a similar metre may be used.

A full music edition is available for the organist. This incorporates an *Index of Other Uses* which extends the use of the hymns and will be invaluable to those planning the liturgy. The music edition also includes melody and guitar chords for use by music groups.

Contents

	Hymn No		Hymn No
Sundays before Christmas	1	Ascension Day	70
Sundays in Advent	11	Sunday after Ascension	71
Christmas Eve	19	Pentecost	73
Christmas Day	20	Trinity Sunday	75
Sundays after Christmas	21	Sundays after Pentecost	76
Epiphany	25	Conversion of St Paul	119
Sundays after Epiphany	26	The Presentation	120
Sundays before Easter	36	The Annunciation	121
Ash Wednesday	42	Birth of St John the Baptist	122
Sundays in Lent	44	St Peter the Apostle	123
Palm Sunday	54	The Transfiguration	124
Maundy Thursday	56	The Blessed Virgin Mary	125
Good Friday	57	St Luke the Evangelist	126
Easter Day	58	All Saints Day	127
Sundays after Easter	60	St Andrew	128

1   9th Sunday before Christmas: Year 1

1. In the void before creation,
   darker than night,
   hear the great divine oration,
   'Let there be light!'
   From the chaos order bringing,
   hear the hov'ring Spirit singing,
   and the joyous cosmos ringing,
   O splendour bright!

2. Christ, before the world's foundation
   hailed, King and Lord,
   now of justice and salvation
   Author and Word;
   You, the Father's true reflection,
   measure of untold perfection,
   bore for us the world's rejection,
   O grace adored!

3. Word made flesh, so long awaited,
   come from the height;
   Light and Wisdom uncreated,
   burst on our sight.
   Come to lighten every nation
   with the gospel of salvation,
   and throughout redeemed creation,
   let there be light!

2   9th Sunday before Christmas: Year 2

1. Great Creator-God, we praise you
   for the beauty you have made;
   for the wonder of creation,
   where your glory is displayed.
   How the universe would prosper,
   were your purposes obeyed!

2. O the glorious revelation
   of creation robed in light,
   'Holy, holy, holy!' singing,
   clothed in peace, with justice bright;
   perfect praise for ever soaring
   like an eagle in its flight!

3. Come, O God, to re-create us,
   pour your Spirit from above;
   bring to birth the new creation,
   long-conceived in holy love,
   born of water and the Spirit,
   life's eternal joy to prove.

3   8th Sunday before Christmas: Year 1

1. O God, forgive the sins of Cain
   which all your people sadly own,
   who stain the earth with righteous blood,
   and make the whole creation groan!

2. We, too, descend from one who first
   the image all-divine forgot,
   and all too often we have said,
   'My brother's keeper I am not!'

3. O blessèd Father, give us grace;
   this stigma we would rise above.
   We long to share the greater scars
   of Christ-like self-denying love!

4. Eternal Saviour, come in grace
   to us who bear this taint of sin.
   Renew your Spirit in our hearts,
   and cleanse the vessels from within.

4   8th Sunday before Christmas: Year 2

1. Forgive, O God, the sinful pride
   which longs for self-exalting power,
   the shame we vainly seek to hide,
   the greed which makes creation sour.

2. The power of sin is fully shown
   by virtue of the holy law.
   O let your saving grace be known,
   and all our fallen lives restore.

3. The Word has come in perfect grace,
   and judgement has been brought to sight;
   new life and hope let us embrace,
   and live in truth's revealing light.

5   7th Sunday before Christmas: Year 1

1. To Abram's God be glory,
   and everlasting praise,
   for his eternal story
   retold since ancient days:
   the promise of salvation,
   and hope of blessings rare,
   a sign for every nation
   who Abram's journey share.

2. The promises of heaven
   we have by faith alone,
   for all the statutes given
   for sin could not atone.
   Yet we, this grace receiving,
   are fully justified,
   the Father's word believing
   who raised the Crucified.

3. The Word now stands before us
   in perfect truth revealed;
   by grace he will restore us,
   our hope in him is sealed.
   And then, in rapture, sharing
   the faith of Abraham,
   we hear the Word declaring,
   'Before he was, *I am*!'

6   7th Sunday before Christmas: Year 2

1. On the sacrificial altar,
   let us lay our hopes and dreams,
   trusting God's eternal promise
   over mortal plans and schemes.
   Faithful, let us make the journey,
   lay the future open wide,
   and, on grace alone relying,
   sacrifice the ram of pride!

2. Called by grace upon the journey,
   justified by faith alone,
   let the faith by words expounded
   be in loving actions shown.
   Faith is more than mere believing,
   and by works of love is proved;
   let us care for one another,
   loving each as Christ has loved.

3. All our values and our knowledge,
   by this sign, are worthless shown:
   he whom craftsmen once rejected
   now is made the cornerstone!
   On the power of love relying,
   all our trust in God we place,
   'til the fruitful new creation
   springs, in faith, from perfect grace.

7   6th Sunday before Christmas: Year 1

1. O Saviour, hear your people's cry;
   release the souls by sin confined,
   and let us, on the journey, use
   not feet alone, but heart and mind!

2. As rescued people, here we stand;
   your thirst for justice may we know,
   confront the fearsome tyrants still,
   until they let your people go.

3. We face the desert road unknown
   with holy awe, but not with dread,
   for truth will be our guiding light,
   and Christ himself our only bread.

4. The faith of Moses now we see
   by Christ, our great High Priest, surpassed,
   and he will lead his people home,
   to see the Father's face at last.

8   6th Sunday before Christmas: Year 2

1. God of redemption, set your people free;
   call us all to justice, peace and liberty.
   Where the strong and greedy still exploit
      the weak,
   come with liberation; grace and judgement
      speak.

   God of redemption,
   set your people free;
   call us all to justice,
   peace and liberty.

2. As from the water Moses once was drawn,
   still, from fear and danger hope and faith
      are born!
   Still you lead your people through the chaos
      rife;
   give us grace to follow, Saviour, give us life!

3. Where fear is rampant, let us choose to be
   signs of hope and wholeness, solidarity!
   Still for peace and healing cries the longing
      earth;
   still, in pain and anguish, hope is brought
      to birth!

9   5th Sunday before Christmas: Year 1

1. Eternal Lord, our strength and refuge,
   with perfect trust our spirits fill,
   to seek you not in mighty thunder,
   but in the murmur soft and still.

2. Your love is known in many nations,
   you consecrate us all as one.
   Here may we grow in faith, fulfilling
   the work of grace by you begun.

3. Come, Son of Man, with pow'r descending
   in judgement and in grace sublime,
   and may your servants here be waiting
   who cannot know the day or time.

4. O pour your blessing on your people
   who long to see your kingdom grow,
   and justice, like a mighty river,
   through all redeemed creation flow!

10   5th Sunday before Christmas: Year 2

1. 'A remnant will return,'
   proclaims the prophet's voice,
   'and those who trust in God alone
   in righteousness rejoice.'

2. Yet evil powers respond
   with terror and distress,
   and, in their dying throes, resist
   the day of righteousness.

3. Let us in trust obey
   our Maker's, sovereign will;

like clay within the potter's hands
accept God's purpose still.

4. For God, in suffering love,
salvation will restore,
and all creation, just and free
will worship and adore.

11 Advent Sunday: Year 1

1. Comes the herald of salvation,
O what beauty in those feet!
Hear the news of liberation,
and with joy the message greet!
Alleluia! Alleluia!
Soon the Saviour we shall meet.

2. So, as those to light belonging,
let us live expectantly,
for the new creation longing,
faith and love our armour be.
Alleluia! Alleluia!
We his risen life shall see.

3. Helpless are the worldly powers,
in the face of judgement sure.
Heav'n and earth will fade like flowers,
but the gospel will endure.
Alleluia! Alleluia!
Full of truth and mercy pure.

12 Advent Sunday: Year 2

1. Look to the heavens above,
and to the earth below,
where in the midst of gloom and fear
the Sign of hope will grow.
The whole creation waits
to see the reign of peace,
when God shall come in saving power,
and all injustice cease.

2. We may be free indeed,
within God's sovereign will,
for those who live in holy love
the law's demands fulfil.
And thus we shall prepare
to face the hour of grace,
and stand, as people of the light,
before the Saviour's face.

3. Here in the present world,
the living Christ we meet,
among the poor and homeless, still
with bleeding hands and feet.
This worship let us bring:
to serve the last and least,
and hear, with them, the Saviour's call
to join the kingdom's feast.

13 Advent 2: Year 1

1. Come, let us turn and hear
the God of all creation,
who freely will forgive
the sins of every nation.
His promise cannot fail,
his purpose will succeed,
and hope will spring to birth,
as flowers from the seed.

2. This promise now is ours,
all grace and truth bestowing;
the word in faith received,
to peace and wholeness growing.
Then let us live by grace,
forsake all vain desires,
and know the perfect peace
which God alone inspires.

3. O Christ, to you we turn,
your word of truth believing,
as sinners yet, by grace,
your promises receiving.
O keep us in your way,
so far our ways above,
and let our only thought
be pure and costly love!

14 Advent 2: Year 2

1. Come, God of creation, to judge and to heal,
and let us rejoice in the truth you reveal.
Tear open the heavens, descend to the earth,
to welcome us sinners as people of worth.

2. The scriptures were written your purpose to show,
that through them all people might prosper and grow.
O fill us with hope, that our faith may increase,
and call us to serve you in justice and peace.

3. Pour on us your Spirit, anoint us with grace,
the poor and oppressed in your name to embrace.
O grant us the vision our hearts long to see,
and let us not rest 'til creation is free!

15 Advent 3: Year 1

1. Behold, the Lord will come!
   Prepare the desert way;
   the valleys shall be lifted high
   to greet salvation's day.

2. With justice and with truth,
   his people he shall feed,
   the humble and the weak embrace,
   and like a shepherd lead.

3. All things shall come to light,
   though hitherto concealed,
   and all the secrets of the heart
   by him will stand revealed.

4. What joyous task is ours,
   to herald and acclaim
   the coming of the living Lord,
   of high eternal name!

16 Advent 3: Year 2

1. The word of hope is heard proclaiming
   the coming of our God most high,
   to fill the world with peace and justice,
   and human nature purify.

2. Still rings the word through all creation,
   'Rejoice! Again I say, rejoice!
   Let pray'r be offered with thanksgiving,
   and truth and beauty be your choice.'

3. The kingdom comes with life abundant,
   with justice for the weak and poor;
   with sight and health, with peace and
     healing,
   so death shall have its way no more.

17 Advent 4: Year 1

1. See the Lord of all creation
   from the line of Jesse spring;
   born of truth and perfect wisdom,
   righteous judgement he will bring.
   Hear the promise of redemption:
   songs of hope the poor will sing!

2. Still in awesome grace and judgement,
   God the humble glorifies;
   those the world derides as 'nothing',
   God exalts, to shame the wise!
   Signs and bearers of salvation,
   'little ones' the proud despise!

3. All the hopes the poor have cherished
   in the virgin's womb will flower,
   and the humble and afflicted
   be exalted in that hour.
   Son of God and son of David,
   Christ the lowly will empower.

18 Advent 4: Year 2

1. Sing, rejoice and celebrate, all things living!
   Health and wholeness, peace and joy,
     God is giving.
   Now the home of God is found in creation,
   and the universe will know true salvation.

2. Sing, rejoice and celebrate life's profusion,
   death itself defeated flees, in confusion.
   Cries of anguish will be turned into singing;
   light from darkness, hope from fear, God is
     bringing.

3. Sing, rejoice and celebrate grace abounding;
   hear the angel's joyful word, still resounding.
   Virgin-born, Emmanuel, we adore you;
   let the whole created world bow before you!

19 Christmas Eve: Years 1 and 2

1. God's delight is in his people,
   we shall be his crown of joy,
   the universe shall witness
   glory nothing can destroy.
   No more lost in desolation,
   knowing life abundantly!

2. Blessèd be the God of Jacob,
   coming with his promise bright.
   He alone will save his people,
   all injustice put to flight.
   Those who waited long in darkness
   soon shall see a glorious light.

3. Hear the word, O waiting peoples,
   children all of Adam's race:
   for the sake of every nation
   God revealed his saving grace.
   See the promise of redemption
   shining in the Infant's face!

20 Christmas Day: Years 1 and 2

1. Now to us a child is given,
   yes, a son is born!
   All the accolades of nations
   will his name adorn!
   At his coming, all creation
   greets salvation's early dawn.

2. Once enslaved in worldly folly,
   we are now set free,
   born by water and the Spirit,
   heirs in hope to be.

His the promise of salvation
every nation longs to see!

3. 'Glory! Glory in the highest!'
hear the angels sing;
God to all his longing people
perfect peace will bring.
Earth and heav'n, their voices blending,
with unending praise shall ring!

21 Christmas 1: Year 1

1. O the word of simple wonder
which the prophets' voices tell!
Hope divine is born of woman,
in this world of flesh to dwell;
born of grace and holy virtue,
God-with-us, Emmanuel!

2. Holy Son, yet born of woman,
under judgement of the law,
still he comes, the lost redeeming,
grace and beauty to restore.
Now as heirs, in blessèd freedom,
Let us worship and adore!

3. Word made flesh to dwell among us,
perfect grace in him is found,
fullness of the Father's glory,
light and majesty abound.
Let the world in silence worship,
O what Mystery profound!

22 Christmas 1: Year 2

1. We bring to you, O God,
in humble dedication,
our lives, our hopes, our joys,
our cherished aspirations.
With ever-grateful hearts,
we lay them at your throne,
for all that we possess
is yours and yours alone.

2. As many, yet as one,
we lay our lives before you,
and, in the love we share,
we joyfully adore you.
Accept us as we are,
by grace our lives remake,
and our imperfect gifts
into your service take.

3. Here may we wait and pray,
in eager expectation,
with longing hearts, to see
the coming of salvation.
Creation shall be free,
oppression's voice shall cease,
and all the waiting world
shall know your perfect peace.

23 Christmas 2: Year 1

1. Great God of love your people hear,
who long your voice to know,
and in each human family
let pure compassion flow.

2. In bread and wine remembering
the freedom you have won,
we celebrate our common hope
by work of grace begun.

3. O God who came from glory's height,
a human home to find,
make every family a sign
of hope for human kind.

4. We worship, by the Spirit's power,
and 'Abba! Father!' cry.
Then may this family of grace
the Godhead glorify.

24 Christmas 2: Year 2

1. Holy God, we rise to greet you,
from the depths of darkest night,
and with heart and voice acclaim you
as creation's one true light.
Kings and queens of many nations
come toward the light divine;
rise in your eternal splendour,
God, through all creation shine.

2. Stars and planets tell your story,
and the wise from distant lands,
seeking ever-greater wisdom,
come with presents in their hands.
All the riches we may offer,
all the treasure we can bring,
cannot match the humble glory
of your own self-offering.

3. Let the glory of this vision
stay forever in our sight,
filling us with hope and anger
where the world remains in night.
In the presence of injustice,
let us never silent be,
'til the world can stand before you,
full of light and liberty.

25 Epiphany of our Lord: Years 1 and 2

1. Called from the very womb,
   and marked by holy grace,
   behold the servant of the Lord,
   revealed in time and space.
   He calls his people home
   to life and liberty,
   and all the nations of the earth
   his glorious light will see.

2. Mystery all divine,
   from angels once concealed,
   now to the waiting human race,
   in flesh and blood, revealed!
   In Jesus Christ we see
   the Father's holy face,
   interpreting to mortal sight
   the purposes of grace!

3. Now to the Presence come,
   by hope and promise drawn,
   to see creation's perfect light
   of grace and beauty born.
   Such simple gifts we bring,
   yet greater far than gold,
   the meagre love and falt'ring trust
   our mortal hearts can hold!

26 Epiphany 1: Year 1

1. O great, all-seeing God,
   our lack of faith you know,
   yet read in our uplifted hearts
   the thoughts we never show.

2. We lift our hearts indeed,
   and joyfully we sing,
   to God who raises up the poor
   and crowns the shepherd-king!

3. But greater myst'ry yet,
   in perfect grace devised:
   the Father's own belovèd Son
   by human hand baptised!

4. O grace beyond compare,
   and majesty unknown:
   to all the world, with none denied,
   your saving love is shown.

27 Epiphany 1: Year 2

1. The servant of the living God
   is seen in humble guise,
   anointed with the Spirit's power
   and worthy in God's eyes.
   He will not speak in angry tones,
   nor kill the struggling flame,
   but justice shall be found on earth,
   and all shall own his name.

2. The way of God is fully shown
   in Christ, who comes in grace,
   to offer every guilty soul
   love's undeserved embrace.
   No effort of the mortal will
   can circumvent the grave,
   but Christ has triumphed over death,
   with power to heal and save.

3. 'Behold, the all-redeeming Lamb!'
   the Baptist's voice proclaimed,
   the Saviour who, in ages past,
   the prophecies had named.
   Anointed by the Spirit's power,
   he takes our guilt away,
   and leads us to the kingdom's joys
   which never can decay.

28 Epiphany 2: Year 1

1. Known of God while not created,
   called and owned before conceived,
   now for service consecrated
   by the word in faith received.
   Let us praise his saving name,
   and his majesty proclaim.

2. Holy God of all creation,
   you the wayward heart have won,
   by the timely revelation
   of the co-eternal Son.
   Show to all the world your grace
   in the brightness of his face.

3. Gracious Father, all-forgiving,
   speaking through the Saviour's voice;
   meet us in our daily living,
   calling us to make our choice.
   In your presence, may we find
   grace and hope for humankind.

29 Epiphany 2: Year 2

1. The call of God, in ancient times,
   was by the youthful prophet heard,
   who opened up both ear and heart
   to hear the life-disrupting word.

2. The first disciples heard the call
   to share the risk of faith and prayer,
   and left their old familiar ways
   to follow Christ, they knew not where.

3. The lawyer, with misguided zeal,
   the road of persecution trod,
   but saw the light and heard the call,
   and took the unknown path with God.

4. God give us faith, with them, to see
   the meeting-point of heaven and earth,
   and witness, at the journey's end,
   the joyful new creation's birth.

30 Epiphany 3: Year 1

1. Glory of the God of Israel,
   radiance of the Lord Most High,
   let us see a hint of splendour,
   veiled to spare the mortal eye.
   Holy Brightness! Holy Brightness!
   Shield our faces, or we die! (2)

2. O the mystery of glory,
   once for mortals' sake concealed,
   now in Christ, the Word eternal,
   to our human sight revealed!
   Alleluia! Alleluia!
   Perfect grace in him is sealed! (2)

3. In the life of all the nations,
   let us see this wondrous sign:
   water too impure for drinking
   you can turn to holy wine!
   O what glory! O what glory!
   Truth and justice here will shine! (2)

31 Epiphany 3: Year 2

1. O God of ancient Israel,
   your glory we declare:
   such undeserving people
   receive your love and care!
   Your grace we do not merit,
   your love we have not earned,
   yet through your faithful presence
   what lessons we have learned!

2. Your ever-present goodness
   in Jesus Christ we see,
   whose hands fed many thousands
   with bread in Galilee.
   The broken Bread of heaven
   in fellowship we share;
   in breaking and in sharing
   is glory past compare!

3. Here may we show your glory,
   from selfish passions freed,
   our own resources giving
   to meet each other's need.
   In poverty and plenty,
   in sickness and in health,
   our life in your communion
   shall be our greatest wealth.

32 Epiphany 4: Year 1

1. God of majesty untold,
   earth and heaven cannot hold;
   with what lowly grace you own
   houses built from wood and stone!
   Listen to your servants' cry,
   ever-humble God-Most-High!

2. Build us as a temple bright,
   filled with your unborrowed light;
   tested in the judgement's fire,
   pure as gold, your heart's desire.
   Christ, our perfect corner-stone,
   you we serve and you alone.

3. Keep your temple filled with prayer,
   sign of love and place of care;
   let us not, for shameful greed,
   profit from another's need.
   Christ, your temple purify,
   and the Father glorify!

33 Epiphany 4: Year 2

1. O God, may we bring
   acceptable praise,
   by hearing your word
   and mending our ways.
   From idols and catchwords,
   you call us to turn,
   make you and your kingdom
   our only concern.

2. In spirit and truth
   we come to your throne;
   in mercy and love
   your glory is shown.
   So shake us and change us,
   surprise us with joy,
   and give us the treasures
   that none can destroy.

3. On earth, may we share
   the worship above,
   of angels and saints
   perfected in love.
   With grace and with justice
   our vision inspire;
   our lives and our worship
   refine in your fire.

34 Epiphany 5: Years 1 and 2

1. God of wisdom and discernment,
   give us grace to know your way,
   loving truth and guarding justice,
   longing for the perfect day.
   Holy God of endless wisdom,
   though creation bears your seal,
   yet your majesty is greater
   than the heavens can reveal.

2. O the glory of your wisdom,
   shown in foolishness divine,
   all the worldly-wise confounding,
   who in passing splendour shine!
   Let us not, for praise of mortals,
   vaunt ourselves in godless pride,
   but rejoice in our belonging
   to the 'foolish' Crucified!

3. Higher wisdom, brighter glory
   than the finest king has known,
   greater than the sign of Jonah,
   in a carpenter was shown!
   Son divine, the Father's image,
   wisdom of the living God,
   let us tread the foolish pathway
   where your wiser feet once trod!

35 Epiphany 6: Years 1 and 2

1. Creator supreme, your glory we own;
   in all you have made, your goodness is shown.
   And yet we abuse it for personal gain,
   exchanging your image for likeness profane!

2. The prophet of old was sent in your name,
   with pow'r to accuse the king in his shame;
   in parable speaking, your wrath he conferred,
   by images veiling the power of the word!

3. The kingdom of God no tongue can define,
   nor mind can conceive the prospect divine.
   In image and story the promise is made;
   as harvest abundant the kingdom portrayed.

4. The Image we see, the story we hear,
   the kingdom we know, in Jesus made clear.
   The Breath of the Father is known in the Word,
   in perfect Communion, for ever adored!

36 9th Sunday before Easter: Year 1

1. The Lord is merciful and kind,
   and longing to forgive.
   He comes to light the humble mind;
   in him the poor shall justice find,
   who in his order live. (2)

2. The servants of the living Word
   no earthly glory find,
   for those who Jesus' voice have heard
   the world's derision have incurred,
   the least of humankind! (2)

3. O blessèd yet are those who scorn
   the glories of the earth,
   for those who suffer, weep and mourn
   shall know the joy of hope reborn,
   O pearl of priceless worth! (2)

37 9th Sunday before Easter: Year 2

1. We trust your word, O God;
   we promise to obey,
   and turn from falsehood and deceit
   to seek your better way.

2. In you is life and hope;
   your wisdom we acclaim.
   Give us the faith to trust your love,
   and glorify your name.

3. Like seed upon the ground,
   your word is freely sown;
   may fruits of righteousness and love
   in all our hearts be grown.

4. This knowledge we would share:
   Christ Jesus crucified;
   the Wisdom of the living God
   in weakness glorified!

38 8th Sunday before Easter: Year 1

1. Let us sing with joy and gladness,
   for the Lord our God has come.
   On the day of his appointing,
   he will lead his people home.
   He will cancel all oppression,
   heal the sick and save the lame,
   in the outcast's heart creating
   perfect praise instead of shame!

2. Here the long-imprisoned spirits,
   paralysed by guilty fears,
   hear the promise of forgiveness,
   music to their longing ears!
   O the wonder of compassion,
   in the Son of Man revealed!
   He who comes in perfect wholeness
   has the lost and broken healed!

3. Now with gladness and rejoicing,
   we this gospel must proclaim:
   God has saved his dying people,
   put an end to fear and shame!

Now the outcast and the sinner
dare to stand before his face,
singing endless alleluias
to the God of endless grace!

39 8th Sunday before Easter: Year 2

1. God of healing power, renew us,
give us grace to trust your word.
Where our lives are scarred and broken,
let salvation's voice be heard.
In the life of all creation
be the healing waters stirred.

2. Let us not, for worldly glory,
vaunt ourselves in vain conceit;
only your abundant goodness
all our needs can truly meet:
grace and mercy all-sufficient,
pow'r, in weakness made complete!

3. Fill us with your true compassion,
blind to colour, creed and race;
love eternal overflowing
into every hurtful place,
'til we see your whole creation
healthy, free and full of grace.

40 7th Sunday before Easter: Year 1

1. Father of truth, to you we turn,
from all our Godless ways,
our worthless idols we destroy,
and you alone we praise.

2. Not as the righteous are we here,
who have no need of grace,
but in the knowledge of our sin,
we seek the Saviour's face.

3. O then preserve our wayward hearts
from all self-righteous pride,
which seeks from humble, thirsting souls
the face of Christ to hide.

4. No longer slaves, but so much more,
joyful and free, we come,
as brothers and as sisters now,
to make our journey home.

41 7th Sunday before Easter: Year 2

1. O God, we share the guilt of all
who have defied your word,
and, from the Source of life estranged,
the call of death have heard.

2. We turn to Christ alone, in whom
your fullness is displayed;
who, through his blameless life and death,
a full atonement made.

3. Preserve us from self-righteous pride,
when others' sins are known;
before we speak about their guilt,
remind us of our own.

4. Then, in the knowledge of our shame,
our broken lives restore,
and send us out, from death released,
to live, and sin no more.

42 Ash Wednesday: Years 1 and 2 (First readings)

1. Worship and praise we bring;
now for an offering,
this we would do:
rescue the hard-oppressed,
find for the homeless, rest,
for where the poor are blessed
worship is true.

2. Here may we set our eyes
on the eternal prize:
justice and peace!
Help us to run the race,
flowing with truth and grace,
'til through all time and space,
conflict shall cease.

3. O let us keep the fast,
growing from first to last
in hope and joy;
and in these solemn days
live in the kingdom's ways;
then shall more perfect praise
our hearts employ.

43 Ash Wednesday: Years 1 and 2 (Second readings)

1. Let us to our God return,
with repentant hearts and minds;
at the throne of perfect grace,
true atonement we shall find.
Slow to anger, full of love,
God is longing to forgive.
Let us to our God return,
and in hope eternal live.

2. Holy God, to you we come,
seeking wholeness and release.
Greed and envy put to shame;
bring our warring spirits peace.
All we need in you is found,
grace abundant as the air!
Holy God, to you we come,
answer every faithful prayer.

3. God be merciful to us,
    for the sin we do not hide;
    let us to our homes return,
    by forgiveness justified.
    Shine the light of perfect hope
    into every darkened place.
    God be merciful to us;
    let us be a sign of grace.

44 Lent 1: Year 1

1. Forgive us, Lord, the sinful pride
   which seeks the highest place,
   and longs to set the human frame
   upon the throne of grace!

2. In such divine humility,
   you seek the way of love;
   but our ungodly pride demands
   a place all else above!

3. When lonely in the desert heat,
   you choose the path of pain;
   let us not heed the tempter's call
   to turn our faith to gain.

4. Our humble praise we now present
   to Christ our great High Priest,
   who leads us through temptation's hour
   to find our souls' release.

45 Lent 1: Year 2

1. Holy God, our great Creator,
   free us from the sin of Cain;
   turn our hearts from jealous anger
   and let love eternal reign.

2. Hear the blood of countless Abels
   cry for justice from the earth.
   Shame the voices still denying
   human dignity and worth.

3. Love of wealth and pride in status
   echo in the tempter's voice;
   let the joy of humble service
   and obedience be our choice.

4. Christ our Priest, once tried and tested,
   you have paid redemption's price;
   for the healing of creation,
   make our lives a sacrifice.

46 Lent 2: Year 1

1. Lord, look upon this world,
   in truth and hope designed,
   but now by fear and conflict torn,
   by malice misaligned.

2. O tragedy indeed,
   our selfish vain desire:
   we fail to see the way of peace,
   and so for death conspire!

3. And yet, the seed of life
   is in the judgement sown,
   and at the very point of death
   your promises are known!

4. Then let us recognise
   the true prophetic word,
   proclaiming God incarnate born
   and Jesus Christ as Lord.

47 Lent 2: Year 2

1. Holy God, behold creation
   now with bitter conflict rife;
   bring us through the storms of chaos
   into order, hope and life.
   Flood the world with holy silence,
   drown the noise of selfish strife.

2. In the conflicts of the Spirit,
   light and darkness, good and ill,
   may the life of Christ within us
   keep us in your perfect will.
   Make of us a holy people;
   all your promises fulfil.

3. Free our tongues to speak your praises,
   open every eye to see;
   from all envy and distortion
   give our spirits liberty.
   Then, in healing love united,
   let us set creation free.

48 Lent 3: Year 1

1. Abraham upon the altar
   lays the dreadful sacrifice.
   As the sign of true obedience,
   he would pay this fearsome price!
   All the promise of the future,
   helpless and endangered lies.

2. But a greater Son and Victim
   is revealed to mortal eyes.
   For our folly, he must suffer;
   from his death will hope arise.
   Now, fulfilling every promise,
   God provides the sacrifice!

3. O the Mystery of ages,
   from the world so long concealed:
   Christ in us the hope of glory,
   now in very truth revealed!

In the suff'ring of the Saviour,
all our glorious hopes are sealed.

49 Lent 3: Year 2

1. Lead us, O God, on the journey of
   faithfulness,
   call us to trust in your promise of grace.
   Teach us to travel together in harmony,
   singing of hope for the whole human race.

2. Christ, who as Word of salvation we
   recognise,
   lead us in faith on the road to the cross,
   speaking of hope at the heart of adversity,
   finding true life at the moment of loss.

3. You who have suffered injustice and
   treachery,
   false accusation and undeserved pain,
   help us to live in compassionate hopefulness,
   firm in the promise that justice shall reign.

50 Lent 4: Year 1

1. The glory of the living Lord,
   on Sinai's mount, was shown,
   though not contained in written word
   on bare, unyielding stone;
   for shining in the prophet's face,
   the light of hope foretold
   that greater Word, that nobler grace
   than law can ever hold!

2. Another time, another place;
   the glory stands revealed:
   the long-awaited Word of grace
   in flesh and blood concealed!
   Here Moses and Elijah stand,
   the prophet and the law,
   with him, whose outstretched, bleeding hand
   their glory will restore!

3. The written word on lifeless stone,
   the face behind the veil,
   await a glory yet unknown,
   which cannot fade or fail.
   The Word incarnate brings to sight
   the majesty divine,
   whose face, with uncreated light,
   eternally will shine!

51 Lent 4: Year 2

1. O righteous God, whose saving power
   in nature is made known,
   let all the world be holy ground,
   wherein your grace is shown!

2. The hope of freedom, burning still,
   like all-consuming fire,
   transfigures every fearful mind
   to share your heart's desire.

3. The light upon the mountainside,
   the questions on the plain,
   may open up our minds to see
   the meaning of your pain.

4. No greater majesty and grace
   could mortal words define:
   the light of Christ, throughout the world,
   eternally will shine!

52 Lent 5: Year 1

1. God of hope and freedom,
   hear your people's cry,
   and on their oppression
   fix your burning eye.
   Fill us with your Spirit,
   we your voice would be;
   let your Word empow'r us:
   'Set my people free!'

2. Christ, we recognise you
   at the heart of pain,
   life-blood freely giving
   for a greater gain.
   Splendid we behold you,
   lifted up on high.
   Let creation, worship,
   praise and glorify!

3. Glory of the Father,
   co-eternal Son,
   let us share your passion,
   and your vict'ry won.
   By your death, release us,
   signs of grace to be,
   and the cry re-echo,
   'Set creation free!'

53 Lent 5: Year 2

1. Restore your covenant, O God,
   in every human heart,
   and let the work of perfect grace
   transcend the lawyer's art.

2. For Christ has come, our great High Priest,
   the sentence to remove,
   and made the perfect sacrifice
   of self-denying love.

3. In humble servanthood he came,
   to be the slave of all,
   and all who would be great must hear
   the challenge of his call.

Verse 4 over

4. Then give us grace, eternal God,
   to share his cup of woe,
   until the world, by grace restored,
   with joy shall overflow!

54 Palm Sunday: Years 1 and 2 (First Set of Readings)

1. Patiently, the servant suffers,
   innocent and free from blame!
   Faithful to his dread vocation,
   his offences none can name.
   O adore him! O adore him! O adore him!
   Bruised, but never put to shame!

2. 'Watch and pray,' the Saviour calls us,
   in his fearful agony,
   but our sight cannot endure it;
   so profound a mystery!
   Senses fail us! Senses fail us! Senses fail us!
   Such a sight, we would not see.

3. Very God, in light resplendent,
   co-eternal Word of grace,
   he who left the heights of glory,
   human nature to embrace,
   now exalted, now exalted, now exalted,
   takes again the highest place.

55 Palm Sunday: Years 1 and 2 (Second Set of Readings)

1. Rejoice! The king has come,
   in awesome majesty:
   upon a donkey's back, he shows
   supreme humility.

2. The nations he will rule
   with grace and judgement sure,
   and with majestic love embrace
   the humble and the poor.

3. What foolishness is this!
   And yet he will prevail,
   in weakness and humility
   when 'pow'r' and 'wisdom' fail.

4. 'Hosannah!' now we cry
   to David's Son and Lord;
   the pow'r of weakness we acclaim
   in God's incarnate Word!

56 Maundy Thursday: Years 1 and 2

1. O Passover of gladness,
   O supper so profound!
   The blood of lambs unblemished
   announces holy ground.
   Aloud, in grace and judgement,
   the God of freedom cries;
   oppression's night is ended,
   and all the victims rise.

2. O night of dark betrayal,
   yet lit by love unknown;
   the Son's eternal glory
   in humble service shown!
   All things to him entrusted,
   he plays the simple role;
   his splendour lightly wearing,
   he carries towel and bowl!

3. The bread and wine he offers,
   'This also you must do,
   and live for one another,
   as I have died for you.'
   In this most simple action,
   the covenant is sealed,
   and all the hope of glory
   in bread and wine revealed.

57 Good Friday: Years 1 and 2

1. Day of wrath and wonder! Who would believe it?
   See the chosen servant in pain and grief revealed!
   Human understanding never could conceive it;
   beauty and glory totally concealed!

2. Yet for us he suffered, bled for our healing;
   mortal sin and sorrow in perfect patience bore.
   Silent, he endured it, our redemption sealing;
   broken he was, our wholeness to restore!

3. Christ, the Son Eternal, in God's own presence,
   offered his perfection to pay redemption's price.
   Love by love begotten, purity in essence,
   he, he alone, could make the sacrifice!

4. Day of wrath and wonder, hope and atonement,
   scarlet-robed we see him, in death with life replete!
   Lifted high in glory, this his great enthronement,
   crying, triumphant, 'All is now complete!'

58 Easter Day: Year 1

1. God is our strength, and for ever will be our salvation.
   Him we acknowledge as Author and Lord of creation.
   Sing and rejoice!

Let all the people give voice!
Praise him with high exultation!

Christ has defeated the tomb which so
    briefly confined him;
death, with its terrible fetters is pow'rless
    to bind him!
Come, then, and see;
know he is risen and free!
Out in the world we shall find him.

Alpha and Omega, Source and Reward
    of creation,
glorious in majesty, robed in eternal salvation!
Come without fear;
life in abundance is here!
Bring him our hearts' adoration.

59 Easter Day: Year 2

1. Alleluia! Christ is risen,
   whom the grave could not confine.
   We proclaim the hope eternal,
   springing out of love divine.
   Alleluia! Alleluia!
   Celebrate with bread and wine!

2. Alleluia! Christ is risen!
   He fulfils our deepest need:
   out of slav'ry, into freedom,
   all creation he will lead.
   Alleluia! Alleluia!
   This our hope, our joy, our creed.

3. Alleluia! Christ is risen,
   bearing life and liberty.
   Human hands cannot contain him,
   for eternal joy set free.
   Alleluia! Alleluia!
   Christ, we praise your majesty.

60 Easter 1: Year 1

1. O glorious Redeemer,
   our strength and our song,
   to you all the praises of nations belong!
   Through sea and through desert
   you lead us to joy,
   and all that enslaves or distorts, you destroy.

2. To faith you have called us; by faith set us free.
   Forgive us our longing to touch and to see!
   The truth so mysterious O let us receive;
   our eyes have not seen,
   yet our hearts may believe.

3. Such wonder, such glory no reason can hold,
   and faith is a treasure
       more precious than gold.
   So may we be tested and proved in the fire,
   and know that your truth is our only desire!

4. O glory eternal, concealed from our sight,
   in splendour mysterious, in majesty bright,
   your people adore you in faith and in joy,
   and, lost in amazement, the Myst'ry enjoy!

61 Easter 1: Year 2

1. Eternal God of hope,
   your people you have fed,
   and, through the wilderness
   to life abundant, led.
   Here may we sing
   your endless praise,
   and gladly raise
   our offering.

2. Eternal bread of life,
   in Jesus Christ, we see,
   who saves us from the fear
   of our mortality.
   Here is the sign:
   our hopes are crowned,
   and life is found
   in bread and wine!

3. Let heav'n and earth rejoice!
   The sting of death is drawn,
   and from the very grave
   is life eternal born!
   So we shall be
   from death re-made,
   in joy arrayed,
   eternally!

62 Easter 2: Year 1

1. Our long-awaited God behold
   in grace and judgement near.
   The broken heart he will enfold,
   and dry the falling tear.

2. Before his face the dead shall rise,
   the voiceless find a voice;
   his light shall shine on sightless eyes,
   and all the poor rejoice.

3. His presence lights the road we tread
   and opens up the word,
   and in the breaking of the bread
   we meet the risen Lord.

4. The Lamb's great wedding feast is here;
   let earth exult and sing,
   and all the great celestial sphere
   with alleluias ring!

63 Easter 2: Year 2

1. Come, holy Shepherd, healing bring,
   and words of judgement speak,
   to those who would exploit the poor
   and prey upon the weak.

2. From every nation, hear the cry;
   in every tribe and race,
   the poor and hungry long to see
   the promised reign of grace.

3. You call the shepherds of the flock
   to lead by love alone,
   expressed in sacrificial love,
   as Christ himself has shown.

4. So give us grace to trust in you,
   and recognise your call,
   until creation lives in peace,
   and you are all in all.

64 Easter 3: Year 1

1. Spirit of God, anoint and bless
   all who obey your voice.
   Call us the captive to release,
   and bid the poor rejoice.

2. Send us the gospel to proclaim,
   word of eternal joy,
   telling of justice and of hope
   which nothing can destroy.

3. Meet us and feed us, living Lord,
   as once beside the sea,
   and in the failures we must know
   your glory let us see.

4. This is the gospel, such Good News,
   burning with wondrous grace!
   Even to faithless eyes like ours
   have you revealed your face!

65 Easter 3: Year 2

1. God of life abundant,
   our poor hearts inspire;
   fill us with compassion,
   and prophetic fire.
   Where the poor are weeping,
   seeing only death,
   let both love and anger
   fill our every breath!

2. 'Life and Resurrection!'
   was the Saviour's claim,
   joyfully re-kindling
   hope's eternal flame;
   'Life and Resurrection!'
   still the Spirit cries,
   and, from dark confinement,
   bids the people rise.

3. In the vision glorious,
   see creation rise!
   Justice is triumphant,
   and oppression dies;
   all distinctions vanish,
   prejudice takes flight,
   and the world rejoices
   in salvation's light!

66 Easter 4: Year 1

1. Let creation raise her voice,
   and with all the saints rejoice,
   for the desolate shall rise,
   perfect in their Maker's eyes.

2. And the once-forsaken land
   shall rejoice to take his hand,
   when the Lord of truth and light
   greets his people with delight.

3. Hear the all-forgiving word
   spoken by the risen Lord:
   'You who failed and fell asleep,
   rise again and feed my sheep!'

4. Let creation raise her voice,
   and with all the saints rejoice;
   hear the knock, unlock the door,
   Christ will pardon and restore.

67 Easter 4: Year 2

Wisdom of the living God,
the life, the truth, the way,
you alone we glorify,
your teachings we obey.

1. Here wisdom stands among us,
   revealed in light divine;
   we break the bread of heaven
   and pour the kingdom's wine.

2. The way of life eternal
   in Jesus is made known,
   by works of love and mercy
   to humble people shown.

3. As pledge of life immortal,
   this sign to us is given:
   the presence of the Spirit
   foretells the joy of heaven.

68 Easter 5: Year 1

Come, let us return
to God who will heal.
Compassion and truth
his presence reveal.
He comes like a shower
of rain on the earth,
with justice and mercy,
and hope of new birth.

The Word we have known,
in figures of speech,
now openly comes
to heal and to teach.
The gospel of wholeness
to us is made clear:
our prayers, with compassion,
the Father will hear.

The Lord will return,
to judge and forgive;
in Adam we die,
in Christ shall we live;
for death, with its terrors
will lie at his feet,
and God reign triumphant
when all is complete.

69 Easter 5: Year 2

Holy God, for ever faithful,
what can keep us from your love?
Persecution, fear or famine,
things on earth or things above?
Loving God, in Christ made known,
you we trust, and you alone.

You inspired the prophets' vision;
in your love secure they rest:
prophets, teachers, saints and pilgrims,
one communion, ever blessed,
who by faith have lived and died,
now redeemed and glorified.

Saviour, keep us ever faithful
in the suff'ring of the earth.
Through creation's painful labour,
bring eternal joy to birth,
when the universe shall be
full of hope and liberty!

70 Ascension Day: Years 1 and 2

1. See the risen Lord ascending,
he who once was crucified,
now in uncreated glory
lifted to the Father's side.
Alleluia! Alleluia!
See his body glorified!

2. All authority and power
now belongs to him alone;
then the gospel of salvation
be to every nation known.
Alleluia! Alleluia!
Everlasting is his throne!

3. Now the Son of Man, in glory,
takes his place with holy joy.
Light of grace and fire of judgement
all oppression will destroy.
Alleluia! Alleluia!
Let his praise our tongues employ!

71 Sunday after Ascension Day: Year 1

1. The Lord is on high, resplendent in light,
with majesty, pow'r, dominion and might.
The fire of his judgement oppression shall feel,
and glory eternal his kingship shall seal.

2. O fill us with grace, and help us believe;
this promise of hope is ours to receive:
the riches and glory of heaven above,
with peace never failing and infinite love.

3. O open the word, its wonders unfold,
of wholeness and life, of myst'ry untold.
Then bless us and send us, your heralds to be,
'til all of creation your glory shall see.

72 Sunday after Ascension Day: Year 2

1. Christ, the very Word incarnate,
God from God and Light from Light,
in a torn, disfigured body,
plumbs the depths and scales the heights!
From on high, his sovereign Spirit
all creation will embrace,
prophets, saints and priests equipping
with the healing gifts of grace.

2. As Elijah, on the whirlwind,
was removed from mortal sight,
so ascends the risen Saviour
into uncreated light.
Through the overwhelming chaos,
Christ has opened up the way.
In the darkness of oppression,
see the light of freedom play!

3. Risen and ascended Saviour,
hear creation's longing cry;
pour upon your waiting people
power which you alone supply:
power to heal the sick and broken,
power, the captives to release,
power to work for truth and justice,
power to live in love and peace.

73 Pentecost: Year 1

1. O Holy Spirit, come;
   as breath, our souls inspire,
   and burn within our cautious hearts
   as holy fire!
   Empow'r our falt'ring tongues
   to speak, in every place
   where language, race and creed divide,
   the word of grace.

2. O Spirit of the Lord,
   your coming we await,
   eternal Helper, Lord of Life,
   and Advocate.
   You are the Father's Breath,
   the Life within the Word,
   the Mystery of truth, by whom
   our souls are stirred!

3. O humble Spirit, come,
   our selfish pride forgive,
   in ways of truth and justice guide,
   and let us live!
   O Spirit of the Word,
   here Babel's curse destroy,
   and all creation make as one,
   in holy joy.

74 Pentecost: Year 2

1. O God, whose majesty, of old,
   was shown in smoke and fire,
   before our waiting eyes unfold
   the glory earth can never hold,
   our senses to inspire. (2)

2. Come, truth and justice to restore,
   with peace and liberty;
   upon all flesh your Spirit pour,
   and let our earth-bound vision soar,
   from fear of death set free. (2)

3. O Breath of God, in every place
   set human hearts aflame!
   Empow'r us by your gifts of grace
   the poor and broken to embrace,
   and wholeness to proclaim. (2)

75 Trinity Sunday: Years 1 and 2

1. Lord, we adore you, Father, Spirit, Son,
   God of triune glory, ever Three-in-One!
   'Holy, holy, holy!' hear the seraphs cry;
   'Holy, holy, holy!' let the earth reply!

   *Lord, we adore you, Father, Spirit, Son,
   God of triune glory, ever Three-in-One!*

2. Great God, exalted in the highest place,
   filling all the temple with your robe of grace
   all the earth's foundations tremble at your voice,
   yet, in perfect judgement, shall the earth rejoice

3. True Son and Father now we recognise,
   whose unfading glory dazzles mortal eyes.
   Through the veil we see you, and our hearts believe;
   your revealing Spirit let us all receive!

4. Father of Jesus, now be glorified
   in diverse creation, fully unified.
   In the Holy Spirit is the promise sealed;
   now in triune glory be all truth revealed!

76 Pentecost 2: Year 1

1. Within this place we gather,
   as people of the Lord;
   a holy, priestly nation,
   by saving grace restored.
   From slav'ry still he bears us
   aloft, on eagles' wings,
   and, in our faithful living,
   a song of freedom sings.

2. Our life is firmly grounded
   in Christ, the living Vine,
   who beautifies creation
   with freedom's heady wine.
   So life in all its fullness
   must our objective be,
   until his name is honoured
   and all creation free!

3. A pure and holy temple,
   built up of living stone;
   a precious, royal priesthood
   the Father calls his own;
   from dark to light he calls us,
   his triumphs to proclaim,
   'til all his free creation
   shall glory in his name!

77 Pentecost 2: Year 2

1. Come, God of justice, truth and peace,
   build up your royal house on earth;
   from mortal fear our souls release,
   and bring the golden age to birth.

2. Keep us as one in heart and mind;
   lives and possessions, let us share.
   Perfect communion let us find,
   one in the fellowship of prayer.

Call us to share the kingdom's feast
with those the world denies a place.
Set us among the last and least,
signs of your ever-present grace.

Glory to God, the Three in One,
whose love can all the world unite,
in whom creation was begun,
and lives in all-embracing light.

78 Pentecost 3: Year 1

Redeemer God, the nations' joy,
the hope of all oppressed,
in you the captives find release,
and slaves their promised rest.

You led your chosen people out
to tread the desert way,
and, safe within your law's embrace,
to follow and obey.

Now, grounded in the living Word,
as branches in the vine,
we celebrate your saving grace,
the fruit of love divine.

Then let us all, made one with Christ,
baptised into his death,
proclaim his word of liberty,
with never-failing breath.

79 Pentecost 3: Year 2

God, our Maker and Redeemer,
all our trust in you we place;
make of us a pilgrim people,
walking in the light of grace.
If in worldly things we prosper
keep us free from worthless pride,
and in humble love and service
let your name be glorified.

When in needless fear we falter,
touching but the edge of grace,
bring us to your loving presence,
hold and heal us face to face.
From the guilt the world imposes,
give our burdened souls release;
speak to us the word of healing,
'Faith has saved you, go in peace!'

When the world, in fear, confronts us,
Holy Spirit, give us breath;
help us sing of life abundant
springing from the heart of death.
Christ, by worldly-wise rejected,
now become the cornerstone,

bring the broken world to wholeness
by the power of love alone.

80 Pentecost 4: Year 1

1. Holy God, you choose and call us
   as an act of grace alone.
   Not for virtue, wealth or merit
   are your special people known!
   Yet, from slav'ry called to freedom,
   your redeeming work we own.

2. Freely may we hold and honour
   your command all else above,
   living for the good of others,
   by the highest gift of love;
   bringing forth, in truth and freedom,
   fruit that will eternal prove.

3. Once as pris'ners kept in darkness
   by the tyranny of law,
   now by faith in Christ delivered
   freely let our spirits soar;
   by the Holy Spirit crying,
   'Abba! Father! We adore!'

81 Pentecost 4: Year 2

1. God of love eternal, we would sing your praise,
   as you seek to lead us in your kingdom's ways.
   God ever faithful, all our sins forgive,
   and in love and freedom teach us how to live.

2. When, on desert highways, pilgrim hearts are stirred,
   let us join their journey, open to your word.
   God ever faithful, call us to embrace
   people of all nations, every creed and race.

3. Reconcile creation, seek and save the lost,
   caring not for profit, heeding not the cost.
   God ever faithful, let your call resound:
   'Join the celebration, now the lost are found!'

82 Pentecost 5: Year 1

1. Lord ever-gracious, your people you call
   from passions and pride
     which enslave and enthral.
   Your life-giving love
     by commandments is shown:
   you call us to love you and to serve you alone.

2. Great are your laws, yet we cannot comply,
   while frightened of living and fearful to die!
   O Christ, in your mercy, our spirits restore,
   to know you and serve you
     in the face of the poor.

3. Saviour, you call us from darkness to light;
   in you is all promise
      and truth brought to sight.
   So help us to live as a people of grace,
   in justice and mercy,
      in the light of your face.

83 Pentecost 5: Year 2

1. God of free, abundant grace,
   all creation you embrace;
   every painful wound you bear,
   and our hopes and dreams you share.

2. Let the love which we have known
   in our daily lives be shown,
   as we faithfully sustain
   those distraught by sorrow's pain.

3. Send us out, with open hearts,
   peace and wholeness to impart,
   and in workplace, street and home,
   let us see your kingdom come.

4. Free us from religious pride,
   let your love be glorified;
   in the Spirit, may we be
   one redeemed humanity!

84 Pentecost 6: Year 1

1. Glory to our forgiving Lord,
   joyful to see the lost restored.
   Let him be honoured and adored.
   Alleluia! Alleluia! Alleluia!

2. Though once alone in distant land,
   now in his presence we may stand,
   seeking atonement at his hand.
   Alleluia! Alleluia! Alleluia!

3. Only this sacrifice we bring:
   patience and love our offering:
   his is the harmony we sing:
   Alleluia! Alleluia! Alleluia!

4. Now let us celebrate the feast.
   God has restored the last and least.
   Glory to Christ, our great High Priest.
   Alleluia! Alleluia! Alleluia!

85 Pentecost 6: Year 2

1. God, in word and action true,
   all humanity renew;
   let us offer worthy praise,
   humbly walking in your ways,
   loving justice, seeking peace,
   bidding exploitation cease.

2. Christ, creation's only light,
   come, restore our jaded sight;
   let us see salvation's dawn,
   all the world in hope reborn;
   joyful in your presence stand,
   healed by your divine command.

3. Holy Spirit, give us grace,
   let us share your love's embrace,
   but in righteous anger speak
   to defend the poor and weak,
   'til, in endless joy, we see
   all the world renewed and free.

86 Pentecost 7: Year 1

1. God in awesome pow'r enthroned,
   O how wondrous is your grace,
   holding your rebellious child
   in the tenderest embrace!
   Hear your people's contrite prayer,
   stay your righteous judging hand;
   lead us, with the bonds of love,
   to obey your just command.

2. O what mercy you have shown:
   debts we never could repay,
   stains no sacrifice can cleanse,
   love divine has swept away!
   Yet, what faithless servants we,
   who such lesser debts recall!
   Open our forgetful hearts;
   let your love be all in all.

3. Perfect love in you we find,
   slow to anger, quick to heal,
   seeking not our faults to show,
   longing virtue to reveal!
   O what majesty is this,
   grace and mystery divine,
   once in pain and death portrayed,
   now made known in bread and wine!

87 Pentecost 7: Year 2

1. Our God, who made the earth and heavens
   is offered greatest praise
   when life is for each other lived,
   in sacrificial ways.

2. We see revealed in every heart
   the essence of the law:
   to house the homeless, heal the sick,
   and broken lives restore.

3. The word engraved on rigid stone
   condemned the world to death,
   but Christ, the Word Incarnate came,
   with life in every breath.

Then let us all in joy embrace
our neighbours far and wide,
and in communities of love,
let God be glorified!

88 Pentecost 8: Year 1

Holy Spirit, help us, we would holy be;
from all self-indulgence set our spirits free.
From fear and envy, work our souls' release,
re-direct our passions, seeking truth and peace.

From all slav'ry free us, let your ways be known;
break the worthless idol, melt the heart of stone.
Cleanse us and heal us, all our souls renew;
keep us ever faithful, loving only you.

Advocate eternal, Spirit of the Lord,
fill us with the graces you alone afford.
Lead us in goodness, let your presence show
in our faithful witness to the Word we know.

89 Pentecost 8: Year 2

Spirit of the God of Israel,
call your church to prophesy;
breathe the joy of life eternal
into our mortality.
Holy Spirit, Holy Spirit,
give us life and liberty! (2)

In the bond of peace unite us,
by your reconciling power;
let not race or class divide us,
for a common hope is ours.
Holy Spirit, Holy Spirit,
bring your many gifts to flower. (2)

In the life of church and nation,
all-redeeming love release;
help us heal the wounds of conflict,
sacrifice ourselves for peace.
Holy Spirit, Holy Spirit,
call the noise of war to cease. (2)

90 Pentecost 9: Year 1

Consecrate your people, Father,
by your true and holy word;
strengthen all whose faithful witness
persecution has incurred.
Make us one, in love united,
hearts by truth and justice stirred.

2. May we wear your special armour,
firm within the world to stand;
truth and wholeness, peace and justice,
hope and freedom close at hand;
faithfully the word proclaiming,
speaking peace from land to land.

3. To your word we would be faithful,
trust the promise you have made.
We believe the God of Moses;
we have seen your pow'r displayed:
pow'r of hope and pow'r of freedom,
perfect love in truth arrayed.

91 Pentecost 9: Year 2

1. We turn to you, eternal God,
in whom our hopes are sealed;
let truth our only banner be,
and love our only shield.

2. We stand opposed to evil powers
of overwhelming scale,
relying on your power alone
when mortal senses quail.

3. Be with us when our faith falls short,
and let us not despair;
remind us of our need of you,
and turn us back to prayer.

4. In slander and in praise alike,
in honour and in blame,
eternal Spirit, give us grace
to glorify your name.

92 Pentecost 10: Year 1

1. What humility is here!
He whom angels all revere
leaves his high exalted seat,
comes to wash his people's feet!

2. Still the humble part to play,
unto death he will obey.
Here is wisdom yet unknown,
now to mortal senses shown!

3. Dare we question what we see;
probe the awesome Mystery?
Only stand in awe and shame,
and his saving love acclaim!

4. Now he rises to the height,
splendid in unborrowed light,
lifted to the Father's side,
and forever glorified!

93 Pentecost 10: Year 2

1. Give us, O God, the mind of Christ,
   humble in thought and deed,
   sharing each other's heavy loads,
   and meeting every need.

2. Open our hearts to those who live
   lonely and full of shame;
   help us to see their proper worth,
   and love them in your name.

3. If those we fear should ever fall,
   pow'rless, into our hands,
   let us not seek for cheap revenge,
   but do as love demands.

4. Give us, O God, the mind of Christ,
   taking the humble role,
   'til, by the pow'r of suffering love,
   the universe is whole.

94 Pentecost 11: Year 1

1. Behold, the servant of the Lord
   in humble love we see.
   He will bring justice to the earth
   and set the nations free.

2. He will not mock, or cry aloud,
   nor kill the struggling flame;
   yet for his law the coastlands wait,
   and all his word acclaim.

3. The Son of man is glorified,
   all others high above,
   and we will be his witnesses,
   by serving him in love;

4. for God has said, 'Let there be light,
   from darkness let it shine!'
   and calls the holy church to be
   a sign of love divine.

5. Then praise the Fellowship divine
   of Father, Spirit, Son,
   the sign of everlasting love,
   the Three for ever One.

95 Pentecost 11: Year 2

1. Build us, O God, as a people of grace,
   and teach us your values to hold and embrace,
   for fairness is measured and justice is weighed,
   but love flows abundant, neither bought nor repaid!

2. Help us discern what is honest and right,
   make truth our commitment and love our delight;
   O teach us to serve one another with joy,
   in peace and contentment which no pain can destroy.

3. Call us to build you a temple on earth,
   constructed from things of unspeakable worth
   to give of our talents, our hopes and our dreams,
   'til peace flows with justice in unstoppable streams!

96 Pentecost 12: Year 1

1. The servant of God
   his word will proclaim,
   and God will restore
   and honour his name.
   With justice and mercy
   the nations he lights,
   and all of creation
   with freedom ignites!

2. His servants we are,
   and friends of the Son,
   who many has called
   to serve him as one,
   in fellowship living,
   his glory we show,
   and all of creation
   his wholeness will know.

3. All glory we give
   to Jesus the Son;
   the old order dies,
   the new has begun!
   To all we announce it,
   invoking his name:
   let all of creation
   true freedom proclaim!

97 Pentecost 12: Year 2

1. To our God let us turn,
   to be healed, and to learn,
   making peace our concern;
   light for every nation,
   wholeness in creation!

   Sing of love and peace,
   sing of love and peace,
   sing of hope,
   sing of truth,
   sing of life eternal!

2. God of life and of love,
   pour your grace from above,
   fear of death to remove,
   hope in Christ revealing,
   broken spirits healing.

Let us be salt and light,
healing wounds, giving sight,
bringing day out of night,
emblem of salvation
for your whole creation.

98 Pentecost 13: Year 1

1. Open our eyes, Lord, let us learn,
open our hearts, with love to burn;
all the oppressed we would sustain,
open to those who give us pain.

2. Love and forgiveness we proclaim;
never shall we be put to shame;
O Saviour, be our advocate,
come to redeem and vindicate.

3. Come, Holy Spirit, from above,
righteous in judgement, and in love;
greater and deeper truth reveal,
and on the kingdom set your seal.

4. Help us the fear and pain to face,
looking toward the throne of grace,
and at the ending of our days,
open our hearts to greater praise!

99 Pentecost 13: Year 2

1. Eternal God, in you we trust,
your greater strength employ,
when forces of injustice rise
to plunder and destroy.

2. You call us, in the place of pain,
to glorify your name,
and with the world's exploited poor
your justice to proclaim.

3. As shrewd as serpents let us be,
as gentle as the dove,
and face the raging of the world
with your unending love.

4. Eternal God, we trust in you,
the only source of power,
and long to hear the world acclaim
salvation's triumph hour.

100 Pentecost 14: Year 1

1. O Father of our family,
be known in every human home,
and let us to this holy place,
as sisters and as brothers, come.

2. We honour mother, father, child,
as each for each a sign of grace;
O let us in each other see
the image of our Father's face.

3. So in the human family
your special love we long to show,
where each, of every age, is held
with firm embrace, but space to grow.

4. All Glory to the Father, Son
and Holy Spirit ever be;
the Sign of perfect mutual love,
the ever-blessèd Trinity.

101 Pentecost 14: Year 2

1. God, our every need providing,
as a parent for a child,
in your endless love, restore us,
heal the souls by sin beguiled.
Let your people be united,
all creation reconciled.

2. Fam'lies both in earth and heaven
share by grace a common name;
by your own indwelling Spirit,
set our jaded hearts aflame.
With the saints, through endless ages,
let us greet you with acclaim.

3. Feed us with the food of heaven,
by your all-sufficient grace;
hear the crying of your children,
lift and hold us to your face;
in the joy of love's abundance,
all humanity embrace!

102 Pentecost 15: Year 1

All the nations of the world
to God alone belong;
this shall be our constant hope,
our never-ending song.

1. In humble love and service,
this world our home must be,
and in our daily living
his image we should see.

2. The leaders of the people
are servants of the Lord;
O may they serve with honour,
in humble deed and word.

3. In nations and in empires
he worked in ancient days,
through unexpected people
in unexpected ways.

4. And still today we see him,
in love and truth made known;
in many forms and colours,
his majesty is shown.

103 Pentecost 15: Year 2

1. For the rulers of the nations,
   God of perfect love, we pray:
   give them wisdom and compassion
   to prefer your kingdom's way.
   May they find, in humble service,
   joys that never will decay.

2. Teach our governments and leaders
   good and evil to discern;
   give them openness to listen,
   and humility to learn,
   then for peace, on freedom founded,
   with a holy passion burn!

3. In affairs of world and nation,
   show us where we ought to be;
   teach us how to value freedom
   and responsibility.
   Never let us rest, complacent,
   'til the world is fully free!

104 Pentecost 16: Year 1

1. O Holy Spirit, fill our hearts,
   let truth and mercy overflow!
   Let unpretentious love be ours,
   and all your life within us glow!

2. In lonely places dark with fear,
   help us our neighbours' wounds to bind,
   and, as compassion's risk we take,
   true reconciliation find.

3. Let us not gain from others' loss,
   or seek the lowly to oppress;
   justice shall be our only joy,
   showing in truth and gentleness.

4. O Holy Spirit, fill our hearts,
   and overflow throughout the earth;
   on our disordered chaos, brood,
   and give the new creation birth.

105 Pentecost 16: Year 2

1. The worship of our hearts we bring
   to God who loves the poor,
   who calls us wholeness to proclaim
   and justice, justice, justice,
   justice to restore.

2. Wherever human love is shared,
   there God, in truth, is found,
   whose love all mortal fear dispels,
   and mercy, mercy, mercy,
   mercy will abound.

3. In love of neighbour, love for God
   its full expression knows,
   when human hearts in peace unite,
   and freedom, freedom, freedom,
   freedom ever grows.

4. The poor and broken of the world
   the face of God will see,
   and all creation will rejoice
   in justice, justice, justice,
   justice flowing free!

106 Pentecost 17: Year 1

1. Gracious God, eternal Saviour,
   Father of the heavenly lights,
   full of truth and firm of purpose,
   in unborrowed splendour bright;
   give us open ears to listen
   to the holy word you speak,
   calling us to act for justice
   and support the poor and weak.

2. Not alone in words of worship
   shall our faithfulness be shown;
   not in grand and lofty buildings
   is your majesty made known.
   Let us sing a song of freedom
   with the outcast and oppressed,
   and, with 'justice!' as our catchword,
   all our lives in hope invest!

3. Saviour, look on us, your people,
   by your healing hand restored,
   called to life in full abundance
   by your loving touch and word.
   Let us hear the call to worship
   in the voices of the poor;
   there, by healing word and action,
   let us properly adore!

107 Pentecost 17: Year 2

1. Let us proclaim the faith we hold,
   by faithful seers and prophets told,
   watching God's promise now unfold:
   Alleluia!

2. God will the nations' peace restore,
   and vindicate the humble poor;
   justice and truth will reign once more!
   Alleluia!

3. Now is revealed the work of grace:
   Christ, in whose love our faith we place;
   healing and hope for every race!
   Alleluia!

We who with Christ were crucified,
by grace and faith now justified,
share in the life by him supplied,
Alleluia!

108 Pentecost 18: Year 1

O Lord, behold your people,
once captive and enslaved,
who freely come before you,
by grace and mercy saved.
With gratitude, we offer
the works of mind and hand,
examples of your goodness
from ocean, air and land.

We come as ransomed people,
a company of grace,
by love of Christ united
in every time and place.
In poverty and plenty,
one common hope we bear;
may we, in true compassion,
both glut and famine share.

In service of the Master,
let us in love exceed
the acts of common goodness
by written laws decreed.
Then may your great creation
to wholeness be restored,
and Father, Son and Spirit
eternally adored!

109 Pentecost 18: Year 2

Holy God, with joy we come
to adore you,
and our overburdened lives
lay before you.
In life's turmoil, give us space
for reflection;
bring your many gifts of grace
to perfection.

With the Spirit's highest gifts
you endue us;
in the service of the poor
you renew us.
With the flame of love divine
you ignite us,
and to share the kingdom's feast
you invite us.

Help us selfless love to share,
freely giving;
in your sacrificial way
gladly living.
Keep us faithful to your word,
strength supplying,
'til the longing world acclaims
love undying!

110 Pentecost 19: Year 1

1. Lord of our fathers, and our God,
   lead us along the path they trod,
   and may our feet with faith be shod, *Alleluia!*

2. Here may we ever faithful be,
   hoping for things we cannot see,
   willing to trust the Mystery! *Alleluia!*

3. Heaven itself, with promised grace,
   makes with the earth a meeting place;
   here we behold the Saviour's face! *Alleluia!*

4. So let us choose to serve the Lord,
   spreading the liberating word,
   making the voice of justice heard! *Alleluia!*

111 Pentecost 19: Year 2

1. God ever faithful give us faith,
   help us to trust in you,
   who, even in the face of death,
   our courage will renew.

2. Despots and tyrants still we see,
   swollen with godless pride;
   yet, in your faithful people's lives,
   may you be glorified.

3. Call us to walk in humble faith,
   where Christ has gone before,
   the hated outcast to befriend,
   and justice to restore.

4. Christ who for sinners lived and died,
   our guilty souls release,
   that we may live the life of faith,
   which offers perfect peace.

112 Pentecost 20: Year 1

1. Our God alone we praise;
   to him our homage give,
   and ever in his ways
   of justice would we live.
   His ways are sure:
   oppression's heat
   may burn our feet;
   we shall endure!

2. We share the way of Christ;
his glory we would see,
who calls us all to bear
his blessèd poverty!
We shall not turn,
but will increase,
with fire for peace
and truth to burn!

3. We hear the Spirit groan;
our suff'ring he will share,
to bring us to the throne
of glory past compare!
Creation longs,
with suff'ring past,
to join at last,
in freedom's songs!

113 Pentecost 20: Year 2

1. Your kingdom, O God, is ours to proclaim,
that people might know and honour your name.
Then give us the courage and faith to endure,
your kingdom establish and freedom secure.

2. Through conflicts of faith you help us to grow;
in struggle and pain, your presence we know.
So meet us, rename us, and call us to strive,
disturbed by your presence, and fully alive!

3. Sustain us with hope, we earnestly pray,
for small is the gate, and narrow the way.
Then bring us with joy to the end of the race,
when freedom and justice creation embrace.

114 Pentecost 21: Year 1

1. We proclaim the kingdom coming;
truth and justice drawing near!
God will vindicate his people,
put an end to hate and fear.
Coming is the God of judgement –
evil flees before his face –
harbinger of peace and freedom,
who will all the poor embrace.

2. Life abundant is his promise,
springing from the very grave!
All the legal codes exceeding,
perfect grace alone can save:
absolute and pure forgiveness
to the undeserving giv'n;
all the noise of human 'justice'
shattered by the peace of heaven!

3. For such perfect peace and justice
we incessantly will pray,
all our hopes and troubles bringing
to our God both night and day.
Praise the Lord who keeps his promise;
praise the Lord who loves the poor;
in the presence of perfection,
let creation all adore!

115 Pentecost 21: Year 2

1. Sing and rejoice, for God is near,
making the glorious vision clear;
putting an end to mortal fear!
Alleluia! Alleluia! Alleluia!

2. In Christ, eternal grace is found,
in whom our highest hopes abound,
out of the grave with glory crowned!
Alleluia! Alleluia! Alleluia!

3. He has fulfilled our deepest need,
from fear of death our spirits freed,
called from the tomb to life indeed!
Alleluia! Alleluia! Alleluia!

116 Pentecost 22: Years 1 and 2

1. The way of God is life and truth,
humility and peace;
we hold his promise in our hearts
that justice will increase.

2. O God, forgive the faithless ways
your people often crave:
those lesser gods which turn our heads,
and point us to the grave.

3. To us poor stewards of your grace,
O Christ, in mercy come.
O be yourself our one desire,
and our eternal home.

4. Our only hope we recognise,
the Father and the Son,
who with the Holy Spirit reign,
the Three for ever One!

117 Last Sunday after Pentecost: Year 1

1. Worship the Lord of life,
who sets his people free,
and leads us from our exiled state,
a sign of hope to be.
He calls us here to live
as citizens of heav'n,
to care about the things of earth
which he by grace has given.

Christ is our Lord alone;
his promises outweigh
the passing pleasures of the age,
which flow'r but for a day.
This is our one desire,
to know the living Word,
and find in him the perfect life
he only can afford.

Worship the Lord of life,
the Father and the Son;
who, with the Spirit glorified,
eternally are one.
This Mystery untold,
our spirits long to see,
and share the life of heav'n on earth,
in growing unity.

8 Last Sunday after Pentecost: Year 2

Our God, we stand before you
as citizens of heaven,
and bearers of the promise
which you by grace have given:
a peaceful habitation,
a dwelling place secure,
where, full of peace and justice,
your kingdom will endure.

The promise of the future
demands that we protest,
where, in the present order,
your people are oppressed.
In places of injustice,
we keep our lamps alight,
and sing of hope and freedom,
amid oppression's blight.

By gracious invitation,
we join the heav'nly throng,
and add our lesser voices
to hope's eternal song,
until the whole creation
shall sing, for endless days,
'To God on high be glory,
and to the Lamb be praise!'

19 The Conversion of St Paul
January 25

Holy God, in mercy save us
from our narrow-minded zeal:
all the light of grace abundant
to our darkened minds reveal.
Then, like Paul, your great apostle,
send us out to save and heal.

2. Free us from our love of status,
and a greater wealth bestow:
give us joy in one another
which alone we cannot know.
From the smallness of our vision,
let your life of wholeness grow.

3. Pour on us your Holy Spirit,
and restore our jaded sight:
let the word of grace and mercy
dawn upon our inward night.
Love shall be our only motive,
and your justice our delight.

120 The Presentation of Christ in the Temple (Candlemas) February 2

1. Come into your temple,
God of truth and light;
sanctify your people,
fit us for your sight.
Banish all oppression,
set the captive free;
fill the world with justice,
truth and liberty.

2. Come into your temple,
claim it as your own,
Christ, though once rejected,
now the cornerstone.
Make us pure and faithful,
never put to shame;
let this royal priesthood
glorify your name.

3. Come into your temple,
as a child new-born;
let your humble presence
put the proud to scorn.
Nations bow before you,
kingdoms rise and fall;
make the world your temple,
Christ, be all in all!

121 The Annunciation of Our Lord to the Blessed Virgin Mary
March 25

1. O Word of grace and truth,
you call us to rejoice:
the sad and poor of every land
have longed to hear your voice!

2. In humble faith conceived
by unexpected grace,
the Light of hope will spring to birth
and rest in love's embrace.

3. Like us of woman born,
   and subject to the law,
   Christ comes to set our spirits free,
   and wholeness to restore.

4. The barren and the poor
   with fertile hope shall sing,
   and with the Blessed Virgin's song
   the universe shall ring!

122 The Birth of St John the Baptist
June 24

1. Commissioned and anointed,
   the holy prophet came,
   to brighten all the nations
   with hope's eternal flame.
   In places of oppression,
   the herald's voice was heard,
   in joyful tones announcing
   God's liberating word.

2. The poor with joy are singing,
   the barren have conceived,
   who heard the gracious promise
   and, full of hope, believed.
   In desert places sounding,
   the voice of judgement cries,
   by God's own word appointed
   to challenge and baptise.

3. The prophet still announces
   the coming of the Word,
   whose message of salvation
   the centuries have heard.
   From David's line descended,
   Christ comes to reign in peace;
   the poor shall be exalted,
   and justice never cease.

123 St Peter the Apostle
June 29

1. Let us choose, in faith, to follow
   where the feet of Peter trod,
   and, through insult, pain and hardship,
   trust the perfect grace of God.
   Where the forces of oppression,
   seek to mute your people's voice,
   come O God of liberation,
   call the captives to rejoice.

2. Christ, the long-awaited Saviour,
   joyfully we recognise,
   holy Word of God incarnate,
   open to our mortal eyes.
   On the faith of this apostle,
   you have made the church secure:
   in the face of greed and hatred,
   love and mercy will endure.

3. Holy God, and righteous Saviour,
   all our hopes in you we place,
   freed from hatred and resentment
   by your work of perfect grace.
   When redemption is accomplished,
   in your presence may we stand,
   crowned with mercy and compassion,
   with the saints on every hand.

124 The Transfiguration of Our Lord
August 6

1. Holy Christ, in light transfigured,
   shining hope upon the earth,
   brighten every place of darkness,
   bring the age of truth to birth.
   Point us to the great awakening,
   when the world in hope shall rise:
   fear and exploitation ended,
   perfect peace shall be the prize.

2. Let us share the heavenly vision,
   hear the great affirming voice;
   in that glorious revelation,
   call creation to rejoice.
   Through the darkness of oppression,
   let the prophets light the way,
   pointing to the peace and justice
   promised on the final day.

3. Come, O Christ, all truth unveiling
   in the glory of your face,
   and our fading lives transfigure
   with your own eternal grace.
   From a thousand thousand voices,
   songs of praise and joy release,
   when the end of fear and torment
   heralds everlasting peace.

125 The Blessed Virgin Mary
September 8

1. Mother of the world's redeemer,
   holy Mary, full of grace,
   sing to us of hope eternal,
   now revealed in time and space;
   and in all the nations' children,
   let us see the Saviour's face.

2. In the humblest of our cities,
   places of eternal worth,
   turn the cries of painful labour
   into songs of joyful birth;

call together all God's people,
from the limits of the earth.

Mother of the world's redeemer,
point us to a greater day:
God will come to live among us,
pain and sorrow pass away.
God will reign in peace for ever,
and the world, with joy, obey.

3. 'Glory to God,' we sing,
'and to the Lamb on high,'
whom, in the Spirit ever one,
we praise and glorify.
You hold in one embrace
the saints in heaven and earth,
who praise your triune majesty
and sing creation's worth.

126 St Luke the Evangelist
October 18

God of perfect health and wholeness,
O what joyful news you bring!
Sightless eyes rejoice to see you,
and the voiceless people sing.
In the desert, in the desert,
see the living waters spring. (2)

From the burden of possessions,
let us find our souls' release;
set us free to travel swiftly
with the word of hope and peace.
Call and send us, call and send us,
that the kingdom may increase. (2)

In the service of the kingdom,
give us faith to run the race:
let our lives be poured and broken,
signs of healing, signs of grace.
Then rejoicing, then rejoicing,
let us rest in your embrace. (2)

127 All Saints' Day
November 1

Firm in the faith of God,
the saints have lived and died,
who with the Son in glory stand,
redeemed and purified.
This is the glorious hope
in which our hearts abound,
to look upon the face of God
with love eternal crowned.

Blessèd are those who thirst
for freedom, love and peace,
who long to see the truth prevail
and all injustice cease.
The humble and the poor,
and all who weep or mourn,
shall rise with all the saints to see
the new creation's dawn.

128 St Andrew the Apostle
November 30

1. Jesus, when you call us, let our hearts
   be stirred,
   open, with Saint Andrew, to your saving
   word.
   Call us and save us, put us not to shame,
   let our faith and service glorify your name.

2. In our daily living, may we hear your voice,
   let the kingdom's values be our willing
   choice.
   Call us and save us, give us grace to move,
   pilgrims on a journey, saved by faith and
   love.

3. Jesus, still you call us, give us ears to hear;
   let this saint's example overcome our fear.
   Call us and save us, send us to proclaim,
   to the poor and captive, freedom in your
   name.

Suggested Tunes for Themesongs
Year 1

No.	Sunday	Suggested Tune	Metre
1	9th Sunday before Christmas	All through the night (Ar hyd y nos)	84 84 88 84
3	8th Sunday before Christmas	New every morning is the love (Melcombe)	LM
5	7th Sunday before Christmas	The church's one foundation (Aurelia)	76 76 D
7	6th Sunday before Christmas	When I survey (Rockingham)	LM
9	5th Sunday before Christmas	The day thou gavest (St Clement)	98 98
11	Advent Sunday	Praise, my soul (Praise, my soul)	87 87 87
13	Advent 2	Now thank we all our God (Nun Danket)	67 67 66 66
15	Advent 3	Teach me, my God and King (Sandys)	SM
17	Advent 4	To the name that brings salvation (Oriel)	87 87 87
19	Christmas Eve	Christ is made the sure foundation (Westminster Abbey)	87 87 87
20	Christmas Day	Angel-voices ever singing (Angel Voices)	85 85 843
21	Christmas 1	Let all mortal flesh keep silence (Picardy)	87 87 87
23	Christmas 2	All ye who seek a comfort sure (St Bernard)	CM
25	Epiphany of our Lord	Crown him with many crowns (Diademata)	DSM
26	Epiphany 1	Breathe on me, breath of God (Carlisle)	SM
28	Epiphany 2	Who are these, like stars appearing (All Saints)	87 87 77
30	Epiphany 3	Guide me, O thou great Redeemer (Cwm Rhondda)	87 87 47
32	Epiphany 4	As with gladness men of old (Dix)	77 77 77
34	Epiphany 5	Alleluia, sing to Jesus (Hyfrydol)	87 87 D
35	Epiphany 6	Ye servants of God (Paderborn)	10 10 11 11
36	9th Sunday before Easter	Dear Lord and Father of mankind (Repton)	86 88 6
38	8th Sunday before Easter	Love divine, all loves excelling (Blaenwern)	87 87 D
40	7th Sunday before Easter	Praise to the Holiest (Chorus Angelorum or Somervell)	CM
42	Ash Wednesday (first readings)	Thou whose almighty word (Moscow)	664 66 64
43	Ash Wednesday (second readings)	Jesu, lover of my soul (Aberystwyth)	7777 D
44	Lent 1	Thy kingdom come (Irish)	CM
46	Lent 2	Blest are the pure in heart (Franconia)	SM
48	Lent 3	Sing, my tongue, the glorious battle (St Thomas)	87 87 87
50	Lent 4	The day of resurrection (Ellacombe)	86 86 D
52	Lent 5	At the name of Jesus (Evelyns)	65 65 D
54	Palm Sunday (first set of readings)	Lo, he comes with clouds descending (Helmsley)	87 87 47
55	Palm Sunday (second set of		

No.	Sunday	Suggested Tune	Metre
57	Good Friday	Holy, holy, holy, Lord God almighty (Nicaea)	11 12 12 10
58	Easter	Praise to the Lord, the almighty (Lobe den Herren)	14 14 4 7 8
60	Easter 1	Immortal, invisible (St Denio)	11 11 11 11
62	Easter 2	Ye choirs of new Jerusalem (St Fulbert)	CM
64	Easter 3	Praise to the Holiest (Gerontius)	CM
66	Easter 4	Let us with a gladsome mind (Monkland)	77 77
68	Easter 5	O worship the King (Hanover)	55 55 65 65
70	Ascension Day	Lead us, heavenly Father (Mannheim)	87 87 87
71	Sunday after Ascension	O praise ye the Lord (Laudate Dominum)	10 10 11 11
73	Pentecost	The God of Abraham praise (Leoni)	66 84 D
75	Trinity Sunday	Thine be the glory (Maccabaeus)	10 11 11 11 and refrain
76	Pentecost 2	Jerusalem the golden (Ewing)	76 76 D
78	Pentecost 3	How sweet the name of Jesus sounds (St Peter)	CM
80	Pentecost 4	To the name that brings salvation (Oriel)	87 87 87
82	Pentecost 5	Lord of all hopefulness (Slane)	10 11 11 12
84	Pentecost 6	Good Christian men, rejoice and sing (Vulpius or Gelob't Sei Gott)	888 and Alleluias
86	Pentecost 7	Jesu, lover of my soul (Aberystwyth)	77 77 D
88	Pentecost 8	Now the green blade riseth (Noel Nouvelet)	11 11 10 11
90	Pentecost 9	Light's abode, celestial Salem (Regent Square)	87 87 87
92	Pentecost 10	Loving shepherd of thy sheep (Buckland)	77 77
94	Pentecost 11	The head that once was crowned with thorns (St Magnus)	CM
96	Pentecost 12	O worship the King (Hanover)	55 55 65 65
98	Pentecost 13	Forth in thy name, O Lord (Song 34)	LM
100	Pentecost 14	O thou who camest from above (Hereford)	LM
102	Pentecost 15	All things bright and beautiful (Royal Oak)	76 76 and refrain
104	Pentecost 16	All people that on earth do dwell (Old 100th)	LM
106	Pentecost 17	Alleluia, alleluia, hearts to heaven (Lux Eoi)	87 87 D
108	Pentecost 18	The church's one foundation (Aurelia)	76 76 D
110	Pentecost 19	The strife is o'er (Victory)	888 and alleluia
112	Pentecost 20	Ye holy angels bright (Darwall's 148th)	66 66 44 44
114	Pentecost 21	Glorious things of thee are spoken (Austria)	87 87 D
116	Pentecost 22	The race that long in darkness pined	

No.	Sunday	Suggested Tune	Metre
2	9th Sunday before Christmas	Christ is made the sure foundation (Westminster Abbey)	87 87 87
4	8th Sunday before Christmas	When I survey (Rockingham)	LM
6	7th Sunday before Christmas	Love divine, all loves excelling (Blaenwern)	87 87 D
8	6th Sunday before Christmas	Thine be the glory (Maccabaeus)	10 11 11 11 and refrain
10	5th Sunday before Christmas	Teach me, my God and King (Sandys)	SM
12	Advent Sunday	Crown him with many crowns (Diademata)	DSM
14	Advent 2	Immortal, invisible (St Denio)	11 11 11 11
16	Advent 3	The day thou gavest (St Clement)	98 98
18	Advent 4	King of Glory, King of Peace (Gwalchmai)	74 74 D
19	Christmas Eve	Christ is made the sure foundation (Westminster Abbey)	87 87 87
20	Christmas Day	Angel-voices ever singing (Angel Voices)	85 85 843
22	Christmas 1	Now thank we all our God (Nun Danket)	67 67 66 66
24	Christmas 2	Alleluia, Alleluia, hearts to heaven (Lux Eoi)	87 87 D
25	Epiphany of our Lord	Crown him with many crowns (Diademata)	DSM
27	Epiphany 1	The day of resurrection (Ellacombe)	86 86 D
29	Epiphany 2	New every morning is the love (Melcombe)	LM
31	Epiphany 3	Jerusalem the golden (Ewing)	76 76 D
33	Epiphany 4	O Worship the King (Hanover)	55 55 65 65
34	Epiphany 5	Alleluia, sing to Jesus (Hyfrydol)	87 87 D
35	Epiphany 6	Ye servants of God (Paderborn)	10 10 11 11
37	9th Sunday before Easter	Breathe on me, breath of God (Carlisle)	SM
39	8th Sunday before Easter	Sing, my tongue, the glorious battle (St Thomas)	87 87 87
41	7th Sunday before Easter	The race that long in darkness pined (Dundee)	CM
42	Ash Wednesday (first readings)	Thou whose almighty word (Moscow)	664 66 64
43	Ash Wednesday (second readings)	Jesu, lover of my soul (Aberystwyth)	77 77 D
45	Lent 1	Hark, a thrilling voice is sounding (Merton)	87 87
47	Lent 2	O the name that brings salvation (Oriel)	87 87 87
49	Lent 3	O worship the Lord in the beauty of holiness (Was Lebet)	12 10 10 10
51	Lent 4	Ye choirs of Jerusalem (St Fulbert)	CM
53	Lent 5	Thy kingdom come (Irish)	CM
54	Palm Sunday (first set of readings)	Lo, he comes with clouds descending (Helmsley)	87 87 87
55	Palm Sunday (second set of readings)	Ye servants of the Lord (Narenza)	SM
56	Maundy Thursday	Hail to the Lord's anointed (Cruger)	76 76 D
57	Good Friday	Holy, holy, holy, Lord God almighty (Nicaea)	11 12 12 10
59	Easter	Praise, my soul (Praise, my soul)	87 87 87
61	Easter 1	Ye holy angels bright (Darwall's 148th)	66 66 44 44
63	Easter 2	Ye choirs of new Jerusalem (St Fulbert)	CM
65	Easter 3	At the name of Jesus (Evelyns)	65 65 D
67	Easter 4	All things bright and beautiful (Royal Oak)	76 76 and refrain
69	Easter 5	Who are these, like stars appearing (All Saints)	87 87 77
70	Ascension Day	Lead us, heavenly Father (Mannheim)	87 87 87
72	Sunday after Ascension	Glorious things of thee are spoken (Austria)	87 87 D
74	Pentecost	Dear Lord and Father of mankind (Repton)	86 88 6
75	Trinity Sunday	Thine be the glory (Maccabaeus)	10 11 11 11 and refrain
77	Pentecost 2	All people that on earth do dwell (Old 100th)	LM
79	Pentecost 3	Alleluia, sing to Jesus (Hyfrydol)	87 87 D
81	Pentecost 4	Now the green blade riseth (Noel Nouvelet)	11 11 10 11
83	Pentecost 5	For thy mercy and thy grace (Culbach)	77 77
85	Pentecost 6	As with gladness men of old (Dix)	77 77 77
87	Pentecost 7	All ye who seek a comfort sure (St Bernard)	CM
89	Pentecost 8	Guide me, O thou great Redeemer (Cwm Rhondda)	87 87 47
91	Pentecost 9	How sweet the name of Jesus sounds (St Peter)	CM
93	Pentecost 10	Praise to the Holiest (Gerontius)	CM
95	Pentecost 11	Lord of all hopefulness (Slane)	10 11 11 12
97	Pentecost 12	God is love: his the care (Persoent Hodie)	666 66 and refrain
99	Pentecost 13	The head that once was crowned with thorns (St Magnus)	CM
101	Pentecost 14	Let all mortal flesh keep silence (Picardy)	87 87 87
103	Pentecost 15	Light's abode, celestial Salem (Regent Square)	87 87 87
105	Pentecost 16	All hail the power of Jesus' name (Miles Lane)	CM
107	Pentecost 18	The strife is o'er (Victory)	888 and alleluia
109	Pentecost 19	King of Glory, King of Peace (Gwalchmai)	74 74 D
111	Pentecost 19	Praise to the Holiest (Chorus Angelorum or Somervell)	CM
113	Pentecost 20	O praise ye the Lord (Laudate Dominum)	10 10 11 11
115	Pentecost 21	Good Christian men, rejoice and sing (Vulpius or Gelob't Sei Gott)	888 and alleluias
116	Pentecost 22	The race that long in darkness pined (Dundee)	CM
118	Last Sunday after Pentecost	The church's one foundation (Aurelia)	76 76 D

Suggested Tunes for Themesongs
Feasts and Solemnities

No.	Feast or Solemnity	Suggested Tune	Metre
119	Conversion of St Paul (January 25)	Christ is made the sure foundation (Westminster Abbey)	87 87 87
120	The Presentation (February 2)	At the name of Jesus (Evelyns)	65 65 D
121	The Annunciation (March 25)	Breathe on me, breath of God (Carlisle)	SM
122	Birth of St John the Baptist (June 24)	The church's one foundation (Aurelia)	76 76 D
123	St Peter (June 29)	Alleluia, sing to Jesus (Hyfrydol)	87 87 D
124	The Transfiguration (August 6)	Love divine, all loves excelling (Blaenwern)	87 87 D
125	The Blessed Virgin Mary (September 8)	Let all mortal flesh keep silence (Picardy)	87 87 87
126	St Luke (October 18)	Guide me, O thou great Redeemer (Cwm Rhondda)	87 87 47
127	All Saints Day (November 1)	Crown him with many crowns (Diademata)	DSM
128	St Andrew (November 30)	Now the green blade riseth (Noel Nouvelet)	11 11 10 11